ALL SQUARE

ROSS HARTSHORN

DEDICATION

FOR MEGAN AND LUCA   XX

HOUSE PLAN

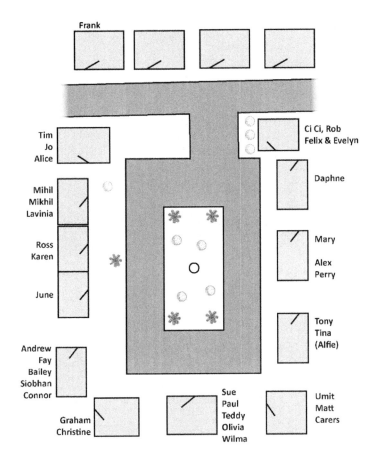

KEY
* Conifer
○ Bush/tree
○ Lamp post

INTRODUCTION

Never ignore the ordinary. Seemingly mundane events each form the link in a chain that can bind everything together and give maximum strength to the unit. Each action in an individual's life has its own story and apparently unimportant occurrences and decisions can make the real difference between success and failure, sanity and madness as well as happiness and misery. This account details the chronology of many such mundane happenings which unfolded during the period of April to December 2020 in a small suburban square comprising 12 houses, the homes of some 30 neighbours. Most of the episodes may appear trivial but, linked together, their chain bound this small community into a harmony and sense of optimism that was desperately needed - not only because of the difficult times brought on by the pandemic but also because of the local upheavals that threatened the unanimity of the community within the square.

CHAPTER 1
THE RESIDENTS

You would think that a house is a house and nothing more. However, this is not true when a group of them become intertwined because of the invisible connections between the people that live in them. Something intangible engenders community combined with a mysterious warmth and welcoming spirit so often lacking in current and established neighbourhoods. Reading this offering, you may grow to understand why this theoretically mundane story has been committed to print and, perhaps, you might appreciate why it is that so many people, totally unconnected to this locality, visit the square in order to assimilate that very feeling of community and wellbeing, even when none of the residents are present.

Community is an aura that all districts should aspire to and, indeed, this has happened in part throughout the country during the deadly pandemic.

This is a square of twelve houses set around a central green space brought to life by mature trees. Houses take up three sides of the square, the fourth side being the open road access to the close - or cul de sac, which is the alternative name used to describe this space. Passing by the entrance to the close is a slightly larger road which connects the rest of the estate and, opposite the entrance, are another four houses which complete the fourth side of the polygon. Built in 1977, these houses not only have seen many changes of residents but also multitudinous home improvements, both inside and out. Somehow, throughout these 40 plus years, there has always been this almost undefinable feeling of belonging and community which, although ethereal, seems genuinely authentic. Over those 40 years the residents have enjoyed countless group events celebrating royal occasions, sporting successes or simply bank holidays. Christmas, however, has always been special. That is the reason why Christmas 2020, a time of incredible difficulty and a period so testing for everybody, has been selected as the theme for this true story.

Straightaway, be introduced to the actual people who inhabited these twelve houses in May 2020 which is when the story begins. Please refer to the house plan on page 2 where you can get a good idea of where everyone lives. Each person in this story has received a well-deserved acknowledgement, they are the ones who make it. Be aware that a book could be written about everybody in every house in this square but not on this occasion.

As you enter the close, the left-hand corner house is occupied by Ci Ci and Rob along with their two children Felix and Evelyn. Rob has been furloughed for some months now while Felix and Evelyn are not in school and are restricted to the house along with their mum. Next door to Ci Ci and Rob, in the first of four houses on that side of the square, is a single retired lady named Daphne. Daphne is an extremely reserved and very private person who suffers from a bipolar disorder, she is separated from her Vicar husband who departed her company one day after the couple moved into the house quite a few years ago.

Next house down is the lovely Mary, widowed some fifteen years ago, a lady who to everyone's amazement is now 85 although she is always very active helping transport patients to the hospital in her car. During lockdown, however, like so many people, she has struggled with her health, a situation exacerbated by the difficulties of getting home medical care when she really needed it. Tony and Tina live next door to Mary, proud grandparents now that their two children have fled the nest. Tony drives a very impressive Ford Mustang, probably the most fawned over car in the entire region. It is a stunning vehicle which is guaranteed to wake up the whole neighbourhood with its lion's roar when it starts up on a "normal" Sunday morning - when Tony, regaled in numerous Mustang logos, is setting out for a car show. However, during lockdown, the sound of silence has prevailed and weekend sleep patterns have been restored.

Over the past few years, the corner house at the bottom of the left-hand side of the square, has been converted into a care home for disabled adults. This residence has around the clock carers in attendance and normally has four occupants, although only two have been present during the pandemic. Ages ago, after some initial months of wrangling between the main residents of the close and the seemingly hundreds of care home staff over where all their cars should be parked, the situation was finally amicably resolved and parking karma returned.

Situated at the bottom end of the courtyard is a detached house with a very narrow front lawn, most of the house's garden space being at the rear of the property. Paul and Sue occupy this house, Paul always works from home while Sue is furloughed at the moment. The couple have two children, Olivia and Teddy, 4 and 8, one exuberant and one very exuberant, if that is indeed possible. Paul and Sue have some difficulty in persuading their offspring to do their bidding, with the "I'll count up to 5" mostly being abandoned at 13 or 14.

The house in the bottom right hand corner has, until a year ago, been occupied by Graham and Christine, their grown up children having left home a long time ago. However, after nearly forty years of marriage, the couple decided to go their separate ways and Christine moved in with her mother who has a flat just around the corner from the square, while Graham continues to live in their house alone.

Coming up the right-hand side of the close, the detached property next to Graham is lived in by Andrew, Fay and their small son Bailey. Their ten years in residence at that house has been a joy to all the neighbours. They are lovely people, so very helpful and kind. Three terraced houses complete the right-hand side of the square, the first one occupied by June, another widow, as quiet and shy a lady as you could ever come across. In the middle house of the terrace live Ross and Karen, a couple with very chequered pasts but who have been together for over 20 years and dote on their two beautiful cats, Megan and Luca. Ross has the distinction of being the only original resident in the close, having purchased his house at its foundation stage and lived in it for all 43 years of its existence. Indeed, he was the very first resident to move in and certainly take root in the square. Karen and Ross, together with Christine, have long been the driving force, if ever one is needed, for any festivities to get off the ground within the close, although spirited helpers are always close behind.

The final house in the terrace is occupied by a Romanian couple, Mihil and Mikhil together with their daughter, Lavinia. This house is a rented property which, to the comfort of all the residents, has always been occupied by lovely people, this family being no exception. The right-hand top corner house is inhabited by Tim and Jo along with their beautiful daughter Alice, 4 years old going on 25. Tim has suffered from health problems for some time now and he and Jo have been isolating since March - and this really does mean isolating - housebound for that complete period, very tough indeed.

To sort of complete the continuity of the square, there are four houses opposite the road entrance to the square, one of which is occupied by Frank, an incredible nonagenarian who has always had very close ties to all of the residents within the square and has been the most valued cat sitter for Ross and Karen. The other three houses on that stretch are inhabited by families who are less familiar to all in the close but, nevertheless, are neighbours to always exchange pleasantries with.

It is against this backdrop then, from the beginning of May 2020 to the end of that tumultuous year, that this story will unfold. It is a tale of 8 months of sadness, hard work, friendship, warmth, celebration, joy and fun which, hopefully, will inspire all neighbours in all communities to nurture the seeds of community sowed during these dark days of the pandemic. What these residents experienced was nothing special or out of the ordinary but, at the same time, it was very special and vitally important to each one of them.

CHAPTER 2
MAY

The end of March 2020 signified a seismic change in the way everybody leads and will lead their lives. By the time the story begins in May, the families in the 12 houses already had been locked away for six weeks, sighting each other only briefly on Thursday evenings during the NHS claps or acknowledging neighbours at a distance with a cheery wave. Even then, not everyone felt confident enough to appear on their doorsteps but absorbed the noise from the surrounding streets through open windows and took great strength from it.

During these difficult times, only Ross and Karen, together, and Andrew separately and on his own would exit the square for the permitted exercise. Andrew is a highly focused and inspirational tri-athlete and his cycling and running training saw him clock up an incredible tally of miles, while new and amateur cyclists Ross and Karen struggled their way up to 10-mile round trips once they had learned to deal with the severe problem of saddle soreness. Their progress to Olympic stature was slightly impeded by a "chain falling off" problem on Ross' bike, but this was soon put to bed by the ever-reliable Andrew who, of course, possessed all kinds of professional bike paraphernalia, including a suspension frame, which enabled him to correct the fault with ease.

Ross, old age unfortunately intervening, was furloughed on 24 March while Karen, a fantastic front-line worker on the tills at Tesco, worked right through the pandemic. Andrew and Fay were both able to work from home, home schooling Bailey between them, but Tim, Jo and Alice, in the top house on the right, had to observe very strict lockdown rules because of difficult health issues, as did Rob and Ci Ci in the other top corner, both families having to deal with demanding problems of home schooling their very talented children. Daphne and June were hermetically sealed away while the lads in the care home had returned to their family residences for safety. Paul had always run his business from home and now Sue joined him by being furloughed and this allowed them to let the children exercise and let off steam outside around the square every few days. Graham, rattling around in his large empty house, was never to be seen, while Christine had moved in with her mother around the corner, although caringly calling into the family home from time to time to check on Graham and, perhaps manage a socially distanced chat with Karen. Tina, working at Dorrington's the Baker, had also worked throughout the pandemic while husband Tony remained safe at home, exercising regularly by polishing the Mustang. Surprisingly, the Romanian family between Karen's and Tim's who worked as domestic cleaners, were able to continue working for a long period and it was quite some time before they had to remain at home.

From the beginning of May there had been a great deal of coverage in the media about VE Day and the fact that it was the 75th anniversary of that important event. During some long-distance conversations on NHS clap nights, the residents decided that they should keep up the close's long-standing tradition of holding neighbourly celebrations, no matter what the impediments, by staging a socially distanced get together on the 8th May, VE Day. Certainly, there would be gaps in who could attend but this was all about self-belief and esteem. Tim's family had not been seen for weeks. Ci Ci's family were very fearful of any contact while Daphne was the ultimate recluse at the best of times. So it was that, opposite corners and ends of the central grassed square were occupied by Tony and Tina, Andrew, Fay and Bailey, Ross and Karen, then there was June spaced alongside Christine, who had brought along her elderly mother, nice and comfortable in her wheelchair, while ex RAF veteran Frank, 93, trundled across the road on his walking frame to complete the celebration. Unfortunately, Paul and Sue were indisposed that day and could not make it while the Romanian family were at work. Ross and Karen had decorated the trees in the centre of the square with Union Jack bunting and flags, plus the lights left up from last Christmas in the central area. This particular set of lights was always left up to be ready for any celebration that was held by the neighbours during the rest of the year. The VE Day event was completed by everybody bringing out their own special picnic of food and drink, so no excuse for not liking anything. Mary, who lived between Tony and Daphne, was desperate to join in, but her health had suddenly and very quickly gone down-hill and she had been in and out of hospital throughout April, never a good sign. Even on 8th May she was waiting for a visit from paramedics and, as regularly happened, they were running very late, something which definitely affected Mary's mental health. As it was, on this day, Tina and Karen went and chatted to Mary at her front door every 20 minutes and this really helped to make the celebration an inclusive event for her as well.

This was a very ordinary get together, nothing more than 3 hours of conversation and interaction, yet it is beyond estimate as to how much of a void it filled and how desperately needed it was. Loads were lifted off shoulders and a feeling of well-being almost physically descended on everyone, for the first time in ages everyone felt almost normal. As conversations tailed off, thoughts turned towards Christmas. Over the years this square had acquired the nickname of "The Christmas Square" because of the lengths the neighbours went to each year in decorating the close and promoting the Christmas spirit. As said earlier, one set of centre lights was always left up throughout the year for off the cuff celebrations and the current ones were white, as the whole close had been illuminated with white lights for Christmas 2019. At VE Day the decision was made for the lighting display in 2020 to be mostly coloured lights abbreviated by sections of white lighting to gain maximum effect. This would mean that the existing lights in the centre had to be removed and the whole canvass would be designed again from scratch.

Decisions made that day included a new pivotal role for the 5ft tall singing Santa, equipped as he was with 6 charming Christmas songs and carols, previously he rarely having been seen because of his susceptibility to the vagaries of the weather. Also, a new grotto would be built for the 6ft tall LED illuminated snowman, a very popular fixture, without the grotto, for the past 7 years. Consequently, the blueprint for Christmas 2020 began its life on that day in May and, as everyone returned to their lockdown lives, there was a future to look forward to.

CHAPTER 3
JUNE

As the calendar turned its page into June and the weather continued in glorious vain, Karen suggested to Ross that work on the Christmas decorations in the square should begin forthwith. This was incredible in itself because Karen was always quick to shut down any mention of Christmas decorations by Ross because of the intolerable pressure she felt on herself when this subject came up every year. However, rather than operating in the cold and damp conditions that Saturdays in October and November usually offered, she had decided that the opportunities presented by the midweek furlough and the fantastic weather were just too good to disregard. The first part of the project involved removing from the central area of the square any lights that remained from the 2019 display, thus providing the blank canvass which then could be nurtured into yet another entrancing display. It was quite a tricky job to remove the existing lights, comprising some five different sets, with the number of lamps on each string ranging from 300 to 600, as the strings were intricately woven in between the branches of the trees. The previous year's display had been all white lights so these sets needed to be taken down, checked and then possibly reused as part of the fresh display. A combination of different ladders and steps, extreme stretching and interminable patience ensured that the whole area was light free by the end of a single day. Karen and Ross were both wracked with considerable aches and pains but were most contented with their day's work.

Right now, Christmas 2020 was underway and the start of the project had provided a great boost to Ross and Karen's mental health as well as that of all the neighbours who only could supervise the work from behind the glass of their windows as they treasured the thought of the celebration that was actually on its way. This simple sign of activity gave people the reason to indulge in socially distanced chats at a time when they were not seeing the outside world for days on end, and those chats snowballed and lifted spirits.

At the VE Day celebrations several ideas had been mooted by the residents about how to decorate the square, the main thread being that there should be a dominance of coloured lights combined with a desire to find an innovative method of illuminating the tree lined central grassed area. As the frontages of the houses surrounding the square really only lent themselves to a pretty basic perimeter illumination, the aim was for that central area to provide a stunning focus for the display. The design that was hit upon was to use the lamp post, which was standing proudly right in the middle of the green area, as the hub of a wheel effect, a hub from which spokes of light would radiate outwards to the edges of the trees on the boundary of the square, producing the effect of a canopy of multicoloured lights. Because this design would make it difficult to access the powerful light at the top of the lamp post, a light spreading source that was always controlled at the last minute before the big switch on by covering it with a thick canvass garden waste sack. They had to ensure that, before the wheel hub project began, any high obstructing tree branches were removed so that the bag could be manoeuvred without difficulty in what would become a rather restricted space. Here Andrew's long branch trimming implement was invaluable and, from the top of an eight-tread pair of steps, skilfully he was able to remove all the problematic branches from around the top of the lamp post area. The dampening of the powerful central light was always the final action before turning on the alternative illuminations because, without that light, the whole area would be pitch black, a situation obviously reversed by the ignition of in excess of 15,000 small LED lamps in the Christmas display. With that likely future problem happily addressed, a two-day inventory and equipment check ensued to determine just how many viable strings of lights were available for use. Some had been old faithfuls for years and it was necessary to know if they were still ok, untangleable and ready for action.

Together with a few new and unused sets of lights there were about 20 sets in all, comprising 14 coloured sets with the rest white. The majority of the strings had 1,000 lamps while the remainder had between 300 and 600, giving a total of over 15,000 light sources. It was all systems go for transforming the central space.

For the central wheel of light, the very clever idea, brainchild of Karen of course, was to use a jubilee clip - a circular pipe joiner, here used as a fixing - to go round the highest point of the pole of the lamp post. This would provide an emanation point for the light spokes of the wheel. Within that jubilee clip, between the lamp post and the clip itself, were placed 50 cable ties, yet to be looped and closed but ready to receive and contain the strings of lights as they journeyed back and forth to and from the edge of the central square. Each journey would range from three to six metres, depending on which edge or corner they were reaching so, with 100 such trips, about 400 metres of lighting strings would be required. Four strings of 1,000 lights would do the job, that's 4,000 coloured lights to etch out an amazing canopy effect. It is often said that patience is a virtue, but this was an understatement as for the next three days Ross and Karen, utilising their trusty pair of steps and their extension ladder, while enlisting the socially distanced assistance of Tony from opposite, painstakingly managed to achieve this, hopefully, sensational effect. Although it was possible to power up the lights by using an extension lead, the effect that they created was extremely difficult to assess because the summer nights were, to be honest, not all that dark, and the illumination of the square by the lamp post was very effective. Nevertheless, the consensus was that it all looked pretty good and that this was the beginning of something special.

Again, what was palpably noticeable was that, even though everybody in the square basically was locked away, from behind their windows they were witnessing joyful activity and a sense of fun that engendered a silent yet real feeling of excitement illustrated so brilliantly by the faces of the children pressed against the glass. This feeling of genuine anticipation further permeated through the residents when the children emerged to partake in their exercise periods and let off steam. Close examination of the initial lighting design was an absolute must to be taken home and reported on. Great for the kids, great and so rewarding for the decorators. Indeed, sometimes Karen and Ross would be working away in the centre area and the interaction between them and the children, Felix, Evelyn, Teddy and Olivia was magical.

Sadly, Alice from the other top house had to live a much more restricted life during lockdown because of the underlying health issues of her dad but every now and again, perhaps during a food delivery, she was able to shout from the front door and tell Ross how much she loved him. What a compliment.

The mere fact that the square as a unit was able to look forwards was so incredibly important towards paving the way for some form of normality to return at some unspecified time in the future. Yet while this generation of optimism was continuing with the Christmas project, sadly Mary's health was rapidly deteriorating. Mary had been a widow for many years. Her two daughters both lived many miles away - daughter Karen and her partner in Margate, (although Karen, tongue in cheek, told everyone that they mustn't call it that but rather, Birchington, the more upmarket end of the town), while the other daughter, Penny, lived up in Scotland with her husband and family. Throughout early June the square's Karen and Tina kept in as close contact with Mary as was possible under the circumstances, both by phone and with socially distanced personal communications, with Karen ensuring that Mary received any supplies she needed from Tesco (where of course Karen was a key worker). Penny and daughter Karen visited at weekends and the two Karen's built up a great bond of friendship, such a massive bonus in so trying circumstances. Unfortunately, as June progressed, events took a turn for the worse and the daughters had no option but to transfer Mary into a hospice for end-of-life care. Mary battled with all her strength to prolong her life and, in fact, rallied very bravely for a few days before tragically she passed away towards the end of June.

Quite unbelievably, it transpired that on the very same day that Mary died, Christine, the lady from the bottom corner house (who was living with her mother around the corner, both of whom had attended the VE Day celebration) also lost her mother to illness. So, after years and years of continuity, the blessings of "no change" were completely shattered by the untimely deaths of two wonderful ladies. Everybody was devastated by this sudden and deeply moving chain of events and the shadows of the whole situation engulfing the country darkened significantly in their very own special little location.

CHAPTER 4
JULY

The sudden disappearance of Luca (Ross and Karen's 14-year-old ginger cat) meant that July simply carried over the sadness that had brought June to an end. Distraught with worry, Karen put a note through every door in the whole neighbourhood and messaged the dedicated local website to maximise any possibility of finding him. The response and concern were simply amazing and the entire community used their exercise periods to search for Luca – all to no avail. Just as two days of frantic and fruitless searching was drawing to a close Sue, from the very bottom house, called Karen over to her front doorstep. Sue and her little boy, Teddy, had been partaking in a bug hunt, counting the number of species of bugs that could be found in and on the bushes that ran along the front wall of their property. Teddy had spotted what looked like a furry ball tucked away at the back of the bushes, an object only partially visible and one which was tucked up tight against the wall of the house. Without any hesitation whatsoever Karen rushed over to Sue's to examine the scene. With simultaneous joy and trepidation Karen could clearly see that the object pressed against the wall was her beloved Luca and he was in a very bad way. Without any thought of protecting her bare arms from the extremely thorny thicket, she parted the foliage to reveal an obviously severely injured Luca with his little face up against the brickwork. As Karen reached into the bushes to lift him to safety, the howl of pain and suffering echoed around the cul de sac and the emotional response from Karen, Sue and Teddy was impossible to contain. As Ross joined the women to hold back the branches and Karen lifted Luca into the clear, the crescendo of high-pitched wailing continued unabated. Luca evidently had been involved in some kind of accident with a vehicle but how he had ended up at the bottom of the square at Sue and Paul's only he would know.

It was plain to see that the damage to his poor body was at the back end and he needed to be got to the vets as a matter of extreme urgency, especially as doubtlessly he had been under the bushes for some considerable time awaiting, as cats seem to do, an inevitable end. It was 8 o'clock in the evening and this meant an emergency admission to the vets - in other words £300 to get through the door. Covid further complicated matters as the delivery of Luca to the animal hospital had to be completed in a Covid secure manner, with the correct social distancing protocol which involved leaving Luca, who Karen had managed to make comfortable in his cat box, outside the building to be collected. Once safely inside, communication could then take place on the phone and the immediate news that Luca's pain could be brought under control was a source of massive relief to Karen and Ross. The next bit of news was not quite so good as the couple were told that an initial emergency X-Ray would cost £600, with the alternative being for Luca to accept his fate as an accident victim. This was a definite non-starter and instructions were given to the vet to spare no efforts in saving this wonderful pussy cat. All the neighbours waited with bated breath for news of the patient's condition and were delighted that at least he would have a chance of recovery. So it was that all the protagonists in this excruciating event could go to bed with a bit of hope, although sleeping may have been a problem.

Next day's vet bulletin imparted the information that Luca had sustained fractures to both of his back legs, as well as significant damage to both hip joints. Luckily, no organ damage was apparent and with proper medical care and a complex operation Luca could make a full recovery. The cost – an additional £3,000 for starters. The decision about this wonderful cat's future was down to Ross and Karen. Was he worth it?

OF COURSE HE WAS!

The operation went ahead forthwith, a procedure which meant the insertion of six screws in one hip and three in the other which, when combined with small steel plates, also repaired the fractures. Most important was – no pain. The procedure was a success and Luca returned home before the end of the month. Here he would spend the next 3 months in "cage rest", a real test of his patience and fascinating for Ross and Karen as Luca developed a serious love hate relationship with his litter tray. Uninjured, Luca had never needed a litter tray, always availing himself of the great outdoors. This, however, was a whole new experience for him and he delighted in flinging the litter all around the lounge - yes, he was looked after in the most luxurious part of the house. The mesh of the cage was no barrier to the flying debris and it was incredible how many corners it reached, even making appearances upstairs. Their other little cat, Megan, found it quite absorbing as to why Luca was in a cage in such a special position within the house and it was great entertainment to watch the two cats interacting.

While the couple were occupied with their feline tribulations, Mary's daughters, Karen and Penny, had to deal with the situation concerning Mary's house. Clearly it would need to be sold but, as well as having to decide on how to proceed with the sale (which estate agent, if any, to use etc) there was also the necessity of clearing the property so that it was in the proper condition to be marketed. With daughter Karen based in Margate and Penny in Scotland, weekday appointments with surveyors and estate agents were very difficult to fulfil. The other difficulty for everybody was the fact that Mary's cat Leo needed to be looked after. He was a really gorgeous animal, soft and cuddly with a lovely nature. Not only did he need care but he also needed to be rehomed. So it was that multi-tasking Karen from the square, became the caretaker, keyholder and cat sitter for Mary's house during this demanding period, while Ross, the labourer, made sure that the gardens remained in respectable condition.

Until you have to do it, it is so hard to imagine just how impossible it is to give away furniture and chattels, even though they are in tip top condition. The Hospice where Mary had spent her last days before she passed away accepted a lot of the furniture, with many of Mary's lovely ornaments being placed in the hospice shop, but other potential recipients sometimes, unbelievably, wanted guarantees and verified kite marks confirming the quality of the belongings that were being donated to them. It was so frustrating that, on several occasions, after the daughters had gone to great trouble to arrange collections from other charitable organisations, when the big vans arrived to pick up the donated goods, the drivers would refuse to take them because the required information labels were not readily visible. Literally they were not prepared to look underneath the furniture or look behind the cushions to check for the necessary marks. As many of these events took place midweek, it was the square's Karen who had to bear the brunt of these excruciatingly perplexing situations while Ross, during this summer of incredible sunshine and heat, had to spend more time watering the lawns than mowing them. The poor daughters had to make many trips to the square over the month of July in order to deal with both the house clearance and to check with "square Karen" that all the professional visits, surveyors etc, had gone well. Finally, with the house now largely cleared, it was ready to be placed on the market. Gratifyingly, a family nearby who had lost their own cat some months previously offered to take Leo in and Mary's daughters were over the moon when they received a video of Leo lapping up all the loving attention in his new home. Mary would have been so pleased.

After some 15 years of complete stability in all aspects of this small community change was definitely on the way.

CHAPTER 5
AUGUST

With Luca on the mend and the shenanigans surrounding Mary's house seemingly under control, Ross and Karen, once again, were able to turn their attention to progressing the Christmas project. Getting electric power to the central grassed area was always a problem. Laying a cable across the road, although the simplest solution, was a non-starter because it was not possible to drill into the road in order to fix a cable protector in a firm enough way to prevent damage to the supply from vehicles. Neither was it feasible to take the power supply from the central lamp post – temptingly straightforward as it was, but illegal and possibly quite dangerous. The solution over the past few years had been to run the power cable via the top of the tall conifer, which was outside Ross and Karen's house, and run it across to the top the tree in the corner of the central square. However, despite some very large and abundantly clear notices warning of low cables, delivery lorries, whose drivers you would think would not contemplate entering such a confined area, consistently managed to pull down the wiring thus ensuring constant work repairing the installation. A new solution was required and, with the time and space offered by furlough, the decision was made to hoist a 3.5 metre length of metal conduit through the middle of the key conifer, its journey skywards beginning some 2 metres up the tree, thus enabling a clearance of over 16ft as the cable passed up through the pipe before being pulled tautly to bridge the 4 metres wide road and then travelling down a corresponding length of metal conduit mounted on the tree in the corner of the central space. Eureka – it worked, you could get a bus under the installation, though surely that problem would not arise. There was a great feeling of satisfaction that continuous power had been achieved, not power that would be obliterated every few days, and it was a joy to have the knowledge that the project could move forward without having to return to square one over and over again. The left-hand row of houses would also need a power source to enable their illumination and this was achieved by Ci Ci, from the top house, offering the use of the power point in her garage, a very simple and straightforward solution, avoiding all engineering difficulties – just plug in and enjoy. So only one lead had to traverse the road and that a great height, it certainly was "all systems go".

Then, without warning, completely unexpectedly, Andrew and Fay knocked on Ross and Karen's door to deliver the announcement that they had decided to move and had put their house on the market. After so many years of tranquil stability it was difficult to process the amount of change that was accelerating through the community. Andrew was at pains to explain to the incredulous Karen that, after so many wonderfully happy years in the square that they had found their dream home. They had discovered it by chance and felt they had no option but to take the opportunity to move. The couple had loved their time in the close and all the neighbours were very dear to them, but a dream home may only appear once in a lifetime and that good fortune simply could not be ignored. The stamp duty holiday just added fuel to the fire of that burning desire, in uncertain times when nobody knew what may lie ahead it had to be a caution to the wind attitude. Just do! The massive bonus for the whole community was that Andrew and Fay's dream property was barely a mile from the square, close to the town centre. Another advantage was that the couple's allotment lay right in the middle of the distance between the two houses, meaning that their allotment would be unaffected by the move and that the supply of courgettes and other tasty vegetables for the community would continue unabated.

Amazingly, Bailey's new kitten Frida, had yet to be allowed out of the house so her confusion would be minimised by another short period of lockdown. So, all of a sudden, after all those years of continuity there were two 'FOR SALE' signs up in the square.

The weather continued to smile down on everyone as the interminable lockdown continued. Waitrose, Tesco, Sainsbury and Ocado deliveries became the norm every day, the vans easily slipping under the super elevated power cable. The cul de sac could experience as many as three grocery deliveries at once and, combined with the Amazon delivery vehicles, the area often resembled the M25 – oh the memories!

Ci Ci, the care home, Sue and Paul, Graham, Andrew and Tim all took advantage of regular deliveries, in particular Graham was well locked away while Tim, Jo and Alice were candidates for the hermit of the year competition. Karen and Tina were the only residents going to work as normal while Rob, Paul and Sue as well as Andrew and Fay were all working from home.

As Karen worked at Tesco on Monday and Tuesday evenings from 6pm until midnight, plus all day on Sundays she was able to perform the shopping tasks for her and Ross while, surprisingly, Daphne, who was a very reclusive lady, actually visited Tesco once a week for her supplies. During the times that she was unavailable at home due to work, not only would Karen leave Ross his daily chore sheet but also provide clear instructions for the continuing work on the Christmas project.

The next stage was to light up the two tall conifers situated on each corner of the top end of the central space, the ones facing the entrance to the close and opposite the 4 houses on the main road which looked in on the square. These conifers, like illuminated Roman pillars, would guard the entrance to the Snowman's grotto, simultaneously protecting and inviting visitors inside for an audience. Hopefully, by 'switch on' time, these houses opposite the entrance to the square would complete the whole effect of the lighting display with their own decorations, squaring the circle or circling the square so as to speak.

The powers that be, ie all the neighbours - via socially distanced discussions as they braved the outside world at different times to show their appreciation of what was happening - had come to the decision that Saturday, November 28 was the date for the Big Switch On and that a celebratory event should most definitely take place.

Everyone hoped that, by then, restrictions would be eased sufficiently enough for the community to really enjoy some sort of festivity.

The big, double 20ft ladder was unleashed from Ross and Karen's back garden and brought round to the front to facilitate the plan necessary to complete the high-level work. Luckily, the conifers were strong enough to support not only the weight of the ladder but also the considerable bulk of its two intrepid scalers. Satisfyingly, after an exacting day of climbing up and down the ladder, cable ties firmly clenched between their teeth, the illumination was complete and, with the power now in place in the central area, both the tall conifers and the wheel effect, achieved early on, were able to be confirmed as working, the multi-coloured configuration a joy to behold, even in the daylight.

CHAPTER 6
SEPTEMBER

As September raised its head, the community would soon be given the opportunity to experience the partial, colourful illumination in the dark, the reason being that not only was it Felix's 9th birthday - Felix being the small son of Rob and Ci Ci - but also it was Tony and Tina's grandson Alfie's 3rd birthday as well. The lights were always switched on for those occasions with the obligatory HAPPY BIRTHDAY signs hung prominently for all to see. This simple action made the boys seem really special and they loved every second of the attention. On each of these two occasions the excitement was well and truly tangible as the young lads wallowed in the photo opportunities eagerly snapped by equally excited family members. Those instants gave the families the chance to escape from their houses and just immerse themselves in a brief moment of the purest joy. Ordinary - yes, mundane - yes, but beyond priceless.

It was an enormous pleasure, besides, for everybody else watching from their windows to take in just how much it meant to these neighbours to have that oh so important release valve. It was a fitting prelude to the big event itself.

It was quite staggering to realise just how quickly time was ticking by and with projects involving the Snowman and Santa Claus in the pipeline there could be no let-up in the preparations. The Snowman's grotto was to be the next item on the agenda, the work starting with the erection of a 10ft square and 7ft tall gazebo, fixed in position by tent pegs and situated in the middle of the central space with its back end hard against the upright pole of the lamp post the lamp which, of course, was now accessible for its light extinguishing cover to be installed as the last job on the list. With the gazebo in position, the next phase of the operation was to illuminate it. 3 lots of 1000 lamp white light strings were to be used to cover the gazebo, hopefully creating a dazzling white grotto for the Snowman to live in, made even more mind blowing because it was situated under that coloured wheel effect blanket of lights. This quite demanding job was almost a whole day's work, but it was oh so worth it.

Now it was that the possibility of the first hiccup to hit the preparations reared its head.

Mary's daughters had arranged for a mega size skip to be positioned on her drive so that they could clear the final unwanted items from the house. The house was on the opposite side of the square to the power cable, so no problem there, but her drive was opposite one of the end conifers which had so lovingly been adorned with its array of spectacular colour. Protection was desperately required in order to prevent the light strings being snagged and pulled down by the skip lorry. Immediately on the case was the incredibly talented and ubiquitous Karen who dug out, from the depths of her shed, a tarpaulin which, with the double ladder again to the fore, was wrapped around the endangered conifer which now became totally ensconced and tucked up in a magnificent protective blanket. This proved to be a 100% effective procedure as the skip arrived, was filled to the brim and more before departing some 10 days later without any ill effects of any kind being experienced by the trusty conifer. Another triumph. All victories, however small, are all vitally important to boost morale and this is true at all times of life and in any challenge.

Mary's house had only just been put on the market but now Andrew's was adorned with its FOR SALE sign as it made its way onto the vending highway. Quite sensationally Andrew had 6 viewings and 3 offers on the very first day of his quest to sell, something that Mary's daughters, Penny and Karen, were stunned by when square Karen phoned to let them know what was happening. Certainly, Andrew had transformed the inside of his property with very innovative designs but his estate agent was definitely more proactive than the one dealing with Mary's house. For Mary's daughters, purple was not a good choice of colour. All the potential buyers of Andrew's property were primed and ready to go, finances in place, and he was therefore in a position whereby he could confirm to the people whose house, a mile or so away, he wished to buy that, indeed, he could now progress his purchase. Things were definitely on the move.

Does lightning strike twice in the same place? Apparently so! Shock waves reverberated throughout the square when Paul and Sue, from the bottom house, announced that they too were putting their house on the market. A decade of nothing now 2 deaths and 3 houses out of 12 up for sale. The transformation seemed as unbelievable as it was incredible. Over the years Paul and Sue had long talked of one day moving into Sue's mother's large property in Nazeing, a property blessed with quite a few acres of land. Their plan had always been to bring up their children in her mother's house while at the same time housing the two sets of parents in more manageable annexes which would be built in the grounds. Covid 19 had simply accelerated their plans. Like so many people faced with this new world order where nobody could predict the future, let alone next day, they decided to act now. There is no doubt that the pandemic had given many people the impetus to do things that they had always wanted to do, perhaps in the knowledge that if they didn't take that chance now it may never come again or, indeed, they may not be around even to have a go at taking it. The couple were now on the hunt for their own estate agent armed with the knowledge of just how quickly Andrew had sold his house.

Staggeringly, after contacting a London estate agent, only hours after the phone call, a viewer arrived and put in a firm offer immediately. Everyone was flabbergasted. It was a fact that all the houses in the square were lovely and that the cul de sac itself was very attractive and generated a fantastic ambiance, but perhaps the reputation of the wonderful neighbourliness of the community went a little way in helping the sales. Those who remained like to think so anyway.

Nothing can get in the way of the Christmas preparations, however, and, on the lighter side, Karen had taken her grandson, Max, who was in her bubble, to visit a Covid safe farm near Chelmsford. One of the attractions at the farm involved the exploration of a very dark barn permeated by the blaring sounds of disco music. Inside, the light show was provided by the children themselves as they had been issued with different colour glow sticks which they waved around like crazy to make very impressive patterns. This was not an idea to be wasted and, as soon as she returned to base, Karen was on the internet ordering glow sticks ready for the 'Big Switch On' on November 28. It was around this time that it became noticeable that neighbours from the surrounding areas were starting to show great interest in what was going on in the square as they passed by on their exercise jaunts. They were used to this close having a pretty Christmas display but they could perhaps feel that this year it was turning into something quite special. It was still only September.

CHAPTER 7
OCTOBER

All of a sudden October had rushed up on everybody and, although brilliant progress had been made in the central square area, with the two tall conifers decorated, the gazebo erected and illuminated and the spokes of the wheel radiating magnificently, lots of jobs still remained to be completed. These jobs included lighting up the back two conifers in the centre, brightening up the two rows of houses on the sides of the square, decorating the big conifer in front of Ross and Karen's house, settling the Snowman into his grotto and, finally, overcoming any problems involved with dealing with the 6ft "indoor" singing Santa Claus venturing to a more hostile outdoor environment.

The left-hand side of the cul de sac was the first job to be undertaken. With the power emanating from Ci Ci's garage, the light string would have its origin in the top left-hand corner of the square, it would start by going backwards, as it were, to cover Ci Ci's porch, which faced the square, and then over the bushes at the side of the house which bordered on the entrance to the close before, at a higher level, travelling back around the corner to move down the whole terrace just below the bedroom windows of each house. Of course, this work involved the big ladder again and it was with his usual trepidation that Ross ascended the ladder to fix the lights in position.

For someone not too good with heights, this was yet another severe test of nerve, something which didn't seem to get any easier no matter how many years of practice of putting up the lights he had put in. For sure that stress levels in this operation reached sky high as Tony's beloved Mustang adorned his drive and definitely had to be immune to falling ladders, debris and lights. Tony's decision to help steady the ladder probably added to the stress levels as any accident would not be able to be explained away with him present on the scene. Happily, all was completed successfully and without incident.

That side of the square beautifully illuminated, the right-hand side was next and, with the power source being the outside socket at Ross and Karen's and a straight line of houses, this was a very straightforward operation, further simplified by the fact that the different house designs meant the lights would be strung at a much lower level, 8 tread stepladder level to be precise. The unpowered end of the string began its journey at the front window of Andrew's house which was now a fair way along the process of changing hands. Then, having followed the upper contours of the property, it jumped across to the top of June's frontage where a convenient drainpipe offered a great fixing point. The three terraced houses, June's, Ross and Karen's and the Romanian family's, were designed in such a way that the deep slanting roofs ended at a level which was half the height of the roofs on the opposite side of the square. At the base of these roofs, a horizontal guttering pipe ran along the soffit board which was just above the front door and ground floor window. With a driveway gap between each house, this was a very easy route for the cables to follow. As said, only an 8-tread pair of steps was required to complete the job, a massive relief for the vertigo infected pioneers recently returned from the high roofs opposite.

The lightshow in the driveway spaces between these houses always provided a very effective display, a display usually enhanced by the addition of a herd of reindeer strategically posted on the lawn in front of Tim and Jo's at the top right of the square. These animals, being nomadic by nature, generally appeared only hours before any main manoeuvres and everyone lived in hope that they would migrate just in time for the 28th.

Tim's herd of glowing white LED reindeer had grown with each year of daughter Alice's life and by now it was assumed that Mummy and Daddy reindeer would have added quite a few reindeer offspring to enjoy the grazing on that front lawn which was shared with the Romanian family. The small bush in the middle of this area also received lighting attention from the main string of lights running along the roofs of the houses and, with the good prospect of the reindeer returning from the mountains, unquestionably this would be an extremely attractive corner of the display.

There was little doubt that a feel-good factor and no little smattering of optimism was gaining strength within the community, still mostly locked away and communicating only in fleeting conversations.

Mary's house had provoked little interest, although it was a fair bit cheaper than Andrew's, both properties being built to the same design. Fair to say, however, that Andrew had, unbelievably, just completed those great home improvements when fate intervened. Good job Andrew loved doing home improvements because he was about to embark on a whole lot of new ones, only on a much bigger scale. Good luck with that!

Following an update from Karen, Mary's daughters contacted Andrew's estate agents, remember he had been visited by half a dozen prospective buyers on the house's first day on the market, the almost instantaneous result being that a couple, unsuccessful in the purchase of Andrew's, arrived to view Mary's property. The almost inevitable outcome was that an offer to buy was accepted by Penny and Karen and all three homes up for sale in the close would all soon be inhabited by new neighbours. Clearly, Mary's property needed work, as an 85-year-old widow she had been very comfortable living in her own cosy surroundings but, with a quite significant difference in price from Andrew's, these buyers would certainly have sufficient funds available to proceed with any alterations they required to put their own stamp on the house. 'Result', as they say.

Andrew was ready to move immediately and had all but completed his own purchase, with a date and a time for both house exchanges set. However, as so often seems to happen in property transactions, a small hiccup in his buyers plans threatened to derail the whole process. Fortunately, things were sorted out and a smooth ride returned to the arrangement and a two-week delay was the reasonably acceptable outcome. Mary's house now took the lead and everything went through quickly and without a hitch. The young couple who was purchasing the house, Alex and Perry, soon arrived in the square to peer through the windows of their new home and get a feel of the atmosphere in the close. Obviously, they had visited the house with the estate agent under Covid 19 restrictions but that would not have been the same as an unfettered tour of discovery and their understandable curiosity certainly had got the better of them.

Step forward Karen, as per usual. Emerging from her house opposite, she ventured towards the strangers and exchanged greetings. To make it a great day for Karen, these strangers had in their company a dog, her favourite animal and, not withstanding her much loved adopted cats, Megan and Luca, she soon befriended 'Peanut', the new pet on the block. Karen, being appointed caretaker on site, had a key to the property and, after gaining clearance by phone to the other Karen in Margate, she was able to allow a very appreciative Alex and Perry access to their own home to be able to fully experience the joy of their purchase. This turned out to be a fantastic opportunity to have a chat with the new neighbours and Tony and Tina from next door also came out to extend their welcome.

Very sensibly, as was the whole consensus, Alex and Perry said that they had decided to do all the alteration work in the house before they moved in and they thought that, probably, they would arrive permanently in the square sometime early in 2021. Perry's father and brother ran a building firm and it was they who would be undertaking the renovations. Mary's driveway would probably have to be visited by another skip, but the couple were by now fully aware of the Christmas project and the need to preserve the integrity of the lights. Of course, Alex and Perry, along with a few guests, were invited to the Big Switch On and they were over the moon to accept. Having previously lived in a flat complex where neighbours rarely interacted, they were absolutely delighted to discover how quickly and easily they had been accepted into their new community. Certainly, by the time the 28th arrived Alex and Perry were already part of the family.

It followed that Andrew, Fay and Bailey would soon be replaced by new owner Siobhan and her son Connor and the neighbours wasted no time in welcoming them to the close as well. Siobhan, like Alex and Perry, would find it quite hard to believe that she was joining such an unusual, at least in these times, and friendly community, and at a moment when a very special Christmas festivity was just around the corner. It was almost a surreal experience for all the new recruits. Paul and Sue had completed their sale as well in what must have been almost record time but they had so many possessions to transfer to their new home that their buyers would not be able to move in until the week before Christmas. Everybody hoped that Paul and Sue would be able to make the Christmas festival but they were spending the majority of their time at the new set up in Nazeing.

CHAPTER 8
NOVEMBER

At this time, the rules dictating behaviour during the pandemic were constantly changing. There was a real and present danger of a new lockdown and a second wave of infections. Tangible nervousness and apprehension were rife and testing the resolve and confidence of everybody not only within this but every community. It was vitally important somehow to maintain and build on the spirit of optimism that had begun to germinate within the square.

As October and November seemed to merge into one month, although quite early in the scheme of things, Karen decided to set up the Snowman in the gazebo grotto. It was a tough enough job getting the chap out from under the stairs let alone trying to remember how he went together.

The man himself, white of course with a black hat, red scarf and green presents, had his own internal white LED lighting system. Beneath the brightly lit grotto he would look magnificent. Luckily, he went together quite easily for the gifted and skilful Karen, the final act being to chain him to the central lamp post. Yes, indeed, even these community events can be so easily disrupted and spoilt by some really unpleasant and selfish people – best to take precautions. The big ladder had to make yet another appearance in order to facilitate the decoration of the extremely tall conifers at the bottom of the central square as they acquired their covering of multicoloured light strings.

The final episode of the coloured part of the extravaganza being the addition of 3000 coloured lights, 3 strings worth, to the big conifer at the front of Ross and Karen's house. The piece de resistance being the addition of a bright white flickering star to the top of the conifer – Bethlehem revisited.

On November 4, a great sadness swept through the square as the removal van arrived to empty Andrew and Fay's house paving the way for Siobhan to replace them that afternoon. To lose such a well-beloved couple from the community was a huge wrench, the upset somewhat tempered by the fact that everybody knew that they were just moving down the road. Change had happened for real.

An invitation to Siobhan and Connor for the 28th was the first thing on the agenda and resulted in another delighted resident who couldn't really miss that something important was afoot in the square. Christmas was only 6 weeks away. The identities of two of the three new neighbours had now been revealed, one set coming in the new year, one set already in. What of the third? Everyone knew that Sue and Paul's house was sold but there was no clue forthcoming as to the identity of the purchaser. All that was known was that the person would be moving in before Christmas. Everyone was just left wondering.

The project only had a few more sub divisions to be completed, the major one being the installation of Santa Claus. The Santa was a Range special, nearly 6ft tall and clothed in a beautiful red velvet suit setting off his long white beard. He had two skills, he could sing and he could dance. His singing repertoire consisted of 6 boisterous carols, each one ending with him saying the immortal words, "Merry Christmas Everybody", while the synchronised movement to his own music probably could be best described as a 'dad dance'. No matter - he was very, very effective.

Asleep in the loft for the last couple of years the first thing to do was to make sure that he retained all his talents. Ross and Karen set him up in their back garden and let him test his lungs with a belting rendition of all his carols. The residents in the close behind the back garden thought that Christmas had come early and joy filled the air as the people joined in with the singing and applauded. Still only November, excitement was building throughout the neighbourhood, a really nice feeling.

With confirmation that Santa was indeed up and running, the next problem, he being designed for indoor use only, was to devise something that would protect him from the elements yet not hinder his ability to entertain. Kings, a large local removal company, kindly donated two very large heavy gauge cardboard boxes to make up a protective lean-to but anything deep enough for adequate protection against the rain could not be built and that idea swiftly bit the dust.

Then, from the very depths of her brain, Karen (clearly someone who should be in government), came up with the second brainchild of utilising the hedgehog run, made from stiff one inch wire mesh, as the framework for a big sentry box type structure. The dimensions of the run were 8ft by 6ft with a 3ft depth. Stood on its 6ft end, this frame was the ideal size to give Santa a fighting chance of defying the wind and rain to mesmerise the children. Very large black plastic building waste bags were drafted in to totally cover the wire mesh frame and make it waterproof, easier said than done - as there was always one seam between the joints of the bags that leaked. Eventually the craftspeople did the best they could and the structure was declared waterproof, secure and ready for action. Declaration isn't necessarily fact though.

When Santa was set up in this open fronted sentry box his home was completed by surrounding him in white lights resembling stars which gave him an even more special aura. Unfortunately, he wasn't heavy enough to stop the wind from catching the structure and blowing it over. Set up on Ross and Karen's driveway next to the big conifer, the sentry box could not be secured with the likes of tent pegs etc. Two long, heavy kerbstones, one for each side of the man in question, were required and acquired, their presence being camouflaged by yet more lights, also white, that was all that were left. As time sped by towards the 28th, the weather had turned very windy and very wet, not very suitable for Santa's velvet clothing, soft beard and intricate electronics, an important part of which was a PIR unit which switched Santa on when it detected movement.

The obvious solution, which the homegrown clever architects had not thought of, was to provide Santa's house with a functioning door. The extra design feature that Karen came up with was a sort of roller shutter, a black plastic sheet fixed to the front lip of the structure to be furled and unfurled over the open front. This not only was used to protect the superstar from the all too regular bursts of rain but also doubled as a security blanket at night. Once again caution came into the reckoning and a complicated chain mechanism secured with padlocks would ensure that Santa did not go on holiday. Sadly, as feared, the design was not quite 100% waterproof and, over the weeks that he was in situ, on quite a few occasions he had to be removed for drying out and hot chocolate. Nevertheless, he soldiered on throughout December and did a cracking good job despite sustaining a few water-inflicted injuries, which were found to be terminal at the end of his showtime.

In what seemed like a blink of an eye from the beginning of this wonderful and amazing Christmas project, the final week before Saturday November 28, the Big Switch On, loomed large. Tim and Jo from the top house were under pressure from daughter Alice to round up the herd of reindeer from the mountains so that they could graze on the lawn outside their house. With no choice but to buckle, Tim gathered up the animals and a beautifully illuminated mummy and daddy reindeer were joined by the original baby reindeer, accompanied this time by quite a few siblings. This glowing LED display of white light sensationally brightened up that top corner of the square and was a brilliant finishing touch to what promised to be a moment worth all the time and trouble.

Mulled wine was next on the list. Although Covid restrictions were going to be observed, the mulled wine urn was not going to surrender its influence on the evening, its warm nectar on a cold November night alone made the party worth attending. The usual consumption figure was around 20 bottles and Karen used her colleague discount card at Tesco to ensure a good price. The urn was released from its box and put together with the bottles and another job was removed from the to do list.

CHAPTER 9
FINAL PREPARATIONS

It is quite amazing when people gather together how great is their desire to enjoy themselves and let their hair down, something that would be even more so following the events of the past year. Also, just as amazing is the simple fact that when people do get together, in spite of that latent desire to let themselves go, almost invariably they are just too shy to carry it through. Reservedness can be such a terrible affliction. Embarrassment is a state of mind. Persuasion and indeed coercion are what is required to overcome these unexplainable nerves. Ross was the man to bring these qualities to the event, he had put his own shyness aside out of necessity a long time ago.

Over the previous years the tradition of singing a couple of Christmas carols had taken seed but this was just off the cuff and sung without music. Now there was time to formalise the singing a bit more and Karen ran off some song sheets so that everyone would know the words to as many carols as Santa. Ross had been asked to return to work at the end of October, such was his great value to his company despite being an old man, and he managed to borrow a super powerful Bluetooth speaker from his work colleague, Gareth. Karen then raided Spotify for backing tracks of instrumental music for the carols that had been chosen, powerful anthems like Hark the Herald Angels Sing and Oh Come All Ye Faithful. The carol service was a goer.

While searching Spotify for carol accompaniment, Karen had come across the energetic old favourite 'The Hokey Cokey'. This held massive possibilities for a socially distanced knees up and she had no hesitation in adding it to her playlist. Ross now persuaded Karen to seek out the instrumental musical backing for 'The Twelve Days of Christmas'. This had been a random success in the past but with careful planning it could be a real hoot. Not long until you find out how all this went down, Switch On was only a couple of days away.

This is what had been achieved: Power to the central space, wheel effect lighting, conifer illumination, the Snowman in his grotto, bordering houses lit up along with miscellaneous trees, Santa Claus primed and ready to sing and dance plus, last but not least, reindeer grazing on the lawn in peace and harmony. Everybody was coming, allegedly remaining in their own space outside their houses and only visiting the centre in turns in order to refill their glasses of mulled wine from the urn or to take a photo opportunity with either the Snowman or Santa. Alice had even managed to persuade Tim and Jo to emerge from isolation which meant that all houses would be represented with the exception of Daphne and sadly Paul and Sue, who had vacated their property on the 26th, although there was no word on the new owner. Christine, still living in her mother's flat around the corner, was the representative from the bottom house and she was bringing along her daughter and two grandchildren.

The new residents from two of the sold houses would be coming, Alex and Perry from Mary's (although not moved in yet) had invited a couple of relatives while Siobhan and Connor would be there along with Andrew, Fay and Bailey who, to everyone's joy would be returning to their old stamping ground from just down the road. Along with Ross and Karen, Tony and Tina, the lads from the care home, June and the Romanian family plus Ci Ci, Rob, Felix and Evelyn, it was a full house of residents together with quite a few guests. Even Mark and Michelle, the owners of Ci Ci's house 10 years ago, came along to enjoy the festivities as they always did.

During that last week's build up, the hoped-for bonus treat was served up as the 4 houses opposite the entrance to the square were all beautifully illuminated by their respective owners, all 4 spectacularly white. There were icicle lights, strings of lights, ornamental trees, the whole wish list which absolutely capped a remarkable effort and completed a breath-taking display.

CHAPTER 10
THE PARTY

The morning of the 28th, arrived and the final act in the saga had to be played out. The bright light at the top of the lamp post had to be extinguished for the next six weeks. Because of Andrew's pruning skills all those months ago, the space around the top of the trees was available to manoeuvre the heavy-duty canvass sack over the light. From the top of the pair of 8-tread steps the target could be reached with the aid of a 3.5 metres length of metal conduit. This long pipe was thin enough to pierce the cartwheel of light strings emanating from that central post and, once it was poked through this light barrier the bag was hung on its end ready for placement over the lamp. Lengths of string were tied to each corner of the canvass sack so that, once covering the lamp, the material could be pulled tight beneath it so that it overlapped when secured and effected a total blackout. In the past, this had proved to be a very tricky job but all the preparations paid off and the operation went like clockwork with a first-time success in achieving complete darkness. However, the sighs of relief could not yet be exhaled. With so many lamps, 15,000 plus, and so many plugs delivering power there is always the worry that the electrical surge at switch on time might trip a circuit breaker so, before any children were out and about, a practice power on took place to ensure that lift off was confirmed. Eureka – success. Bring on the festival.

Luck favours the brave and the night was blessed by the weather gods, a little bit chilly but most important of all – dry. Everyone came out of their houses and into their space at 4.30pm and when the array of revellers was complete, a little bit tricky to confirm in the pitch black, on came the whole shebang of the Christmas spectacular, not only in the square but also on the 4 houses opposite. Absolutely brilliant! Immediately out of the traps came Ross and Karen in order to present everyone with their first disposable cup of mulled wine accompanied by their obligatory song sheet. Karen had added goodie bags of Haribo sweets to her glow stick package and these were eagerly snapped up by both parents and children. Glow sticks for everybody – don't you just love it!

All the expected residents were outside and primed for action as Alex and Perry, with a couple of friends, arrived from Buckhurst Hill and staked their claim outside their newly acquired property. The festivities normally lasted a couple of hours and that was the aim so that people didn't get cold and also left on a high. Karen's music centre provided the background soundtrack for the event with Christmas favourites ranging from Slade to Wham and Nat King Cole to Shaking Stevens blaring out at many decibels. This generated a really festive atmosphere and, as the pent-up excitement began to be released the children expended bundles of energy as they rushed, glowsticks in each hand, from the Snowman to Santa and back again, steaming under the cartwheel of lights in the central square and just drinking the special something that these fantastic illuminations brought to the close. Naturally, as the refills of mulled wine were drained from the urn and people became genuinely excited by the close proximity of their friends and neighbours, little groups did tend to converge, but no rules were really breached. This closeness was accentuated by the flashing glowsticks which both adults and children enjoyed with unbridled enthusiasm. After about 40 minutes of conversation, drinking and general interaction, Ross decided that it was time for the group activities, when genuine Christmas merriment on a very basic level would be demanded from the whole gang. As said, there is no question that people want to get involved and have fun, this desire is buried deep in one and all, but for some unaccountable reason shyness and reservedness simply prevents them from letting themselves go. A fearless leader was needed to defeat all this negativity and, even seemingly against their will, force them to have some fun. That person was Ross.

Bluetooth speaker on, instrumentals of Christmas carols booming across the close, this was the moment to strike. Showing no mercy he commanded the pent-up hordes to raise their song sheets skywards, with his appalling and tuneless (but very loud) voice echoing around the whole neighboured. He led this rag, tag and bobtail choir in a rendition of 'Hark the Herald Angels Sing', their inaugural offering. And by Jove did they sing. They were magnificent and almost in tune. They had fun. From a long way away, distant and rewarding sounds of other people joining in could be rewardingly heard.

No stopping them now! On to 'Oh Come All Ye Faithful' and the other favourites, all belted out with truly gay abandon. People had forgotten just how much pleasure came from singing your heart out, after all - your own voice is blotted out by everyone else's. This all too brief concert was brought to a close by a great version of 'We Wish You a Merry Christmas' and this one was helped along by Santa Claus himself as it was one of his tunes. Now the mulled wine was having a relaxation effect on the adults while the excitement levels of the children were still at fever pitch.

All inhibitions had vanished and it was time for an even more action-based bit of entertainment. 'The 12 days of Christmas' ('Partridge in a Pear Tree' for the uninitiated) presents a fabulous opportunity for both individuals and small groups to show what they are all about. The 12 distinct verses allow the chance of having the whole crowd as the main group to sing the chorus, 'and a partridge in a pear tree', while 11 other separate sub groups or individuals each have a verse of their own to perform. Clearly, the earlier in the song that your verse comes, the more times you have to sing it. The icing on the cake in performing this classic is to encourage the participants to enhance their singing by adding strange and silly actions and gestures to their general presentation.

With everyone well and truly hyped up by now, no difficulty was encountered to make this happen. In this song there is always a battle royal to collar the verse '5 Gold Rings' – it offers such an opportunity to showcase one's talents. Christine, from the bottom house had, in previous years, made this verse her own by singing it with the haunting sweetness, barely audible in fact, of a sweet, if almost silent, soprano voice. She was a star. Tony, the Mustang driving ex rocker husband of Tina, the man with a bejewelled Elvis suit - too small now - in his wardrobe was more into the heavy beat of '10 drummers drumming'. Everyone else just sang what they were given – although by this time the Romanian family were struggling a little bit to decipher what was actually going on. The overall performance was nothing short of sensational with each little group singing their verse with real gusto while every round of the chorus got better and better. What super fun, a little less socially distanced by now but just about ok.

What could follow The Partridge? It had to be the Hokey Cokey! Enjoyment fatigue – no way, bring it on. Would you believe it, anybody under 40 had never heard of this dance, let alone know how to do it. Consequently, before it could get under way, a full lesson teaching the steps had to be given. This gave rise to even more hilarity and the party was really rocking. Completely new to the children, they could not get over just how much fun it was to run towards each other at full pelt when it came to the chorus.

"Oh hokey cokey cokey, oh hokey cokey cokey, oh hokey cokey cokey, knees bend arms stretch rah rah rah!"

What a blast. Although many dancers got their left arms mixed up with their right legs, the whole dance was an amazing success and worth every bit of the tons of energy that was expended. With Santa singing constantly in the background because his PIR was triggered every 5 seconds; with the glow sticks weaving neverending patterns; with the Snowman the supreme ruler of his grotto and the absolute well-being of everyone - the whole event was quite simply the best ever.

Exhaustion made it natural to wind everything down by around 7.30pm and the community had really come together to enjoy a neighbourhood building spectacular. Thoroughly enjoyable, on every level.

CHAPTER 11
DECEMBER

It is hardly surprising that just about everybody in a 2-mile radius got to know, if they didn't already, that something quite extraordinary had gone down in Christmas Square. The boisterous sounds of the singing and dancing would have reverberated all around the entire neighboured and the glow of the lights was visible from every which way you looked. Indeed, this was confirmed a few days into December when a police car was spotted parked up under the lights. As the officers exited the vehicle to stretch their legs, they explained to one of the residents that members of the force loved to come to the square during their breaks to unwind and get a real sense of true Christmas spirit. They also, jokingly, said that they had received worried phone calls from air traffic control, up the road at Stansted Airport, as many of the pilots were getting our Christmas display confused with the landing lights on the runways. Well done, officers.

It was barely a week into December when the mystery surrounding the purchase of Paul and Sue's property was solved. The couple had moved to Nazeing before the Christmas festival and had left no clue as to who would be moving in. It was an amusing situation when, amidst all those blazing lights, the neighbours were all completely in the dark about who would be joining them. The apprehension and waiting were brought to a shuddering halt when the lovely Wilma arrived to take her place in the community. Wilma is a retired lady who lives with her son and she was very disappointed to have missed all the special festivities. No doubt she will have many such celebrations to look forward to in the square in the future.

Accordingly, the word was well and truly out and all through December countless visitors came to enjoy the atmosphere with the younger children really loving Santa Claus whose PIR now ensured that he produced his repertoire only on demand. One very happy lady informed Karen, whose driveway Santa occupied, that she had brought her daughter with her, as she had done every year for the seven years since she was born, and that every year she had taken a photo of her little girl alongside the Snowman. Here she was again and what an historic group of photos she had taken during those seven years. Pure magic. Out of the blue, one Monday morning in December when Ross went into work at Ware, Gareth, (the workmate who had lent them the supremely effective blue tooth speaker), told him that he had visited the square on the evening before, Sunday, with his wife and 2-year-old son. He said that they were in disbelief at what had been achieved and reported that while his family was enjoying Santa's songs and the aura of the Snowman, at least another half a dozen little family groups visited to do exactly the same. What a reward for everyone involved and what a fabulous feel-good factor had been generated.

The social side of Christmas celebrations was cancelled by the government later on in the month. However, the illuminations remained lit until after the New Year and lots of people continued to take a lot of pleasure from them.

This story ends on a massive high though, that will also live long in the memory. This took the form of another surreal happening which, literally, just came round the corner. Each year The Rotary Club runs a Christmas fundraiser involving a live Santa Claus travelling along in a Land Rover converted into a sleigh and pulled by a huge Rudolph the Red Nosed Reindeer. This parade is renowned for its very, very loud Christmas music which is ghetto blasted from the front of the sleigh while myriads of helpers, dressed as elves, take buckets to each house to collect donations. Too big to get around the tight corners of the square, the reindeer led procession manoeuvred its way along the straight road at the top of the square, poignantly coming to a halt at the entrance to this incredible light fest. Under the fantastic atmosphere created by the illuminations, the incredible level of the music and the brilliant animation of the elves and, indeed, Santa himself, not a single household for miles around remained indoors. Parents and children had witnessed something else really quite special and they all believed in the magic of Christmas.

In many ways this story of hope and joy is similar to a parable. Its simple message is that you most definitely get out so much more than you put in. Togetherness, even in spirit, can overcome isolation, desolation and trepidation. So much is to be gained by trying, by supporting each other and by making sure that there is always something to look forward to. When your community is strong and happy, every single second of life really is worth living.

The important word is ... BELIEVE.

Printed in Great Britain
by Amazon

28103386R00036